Kama Sutra

Thorsons First Directions

Kama Sutra

Thorsons
An Imprint of HarperCollins*Publishers*
77–85 Fulham Palace Road,
Hammersmith, London W6 8JB

The Thorsons website is: www.thorsons.com

Published by Thorsons 2001

10 9 8 7 6 5 4 3 2 1

Text derived from *Kama Sutra*, *The Arts of Love*, published by Thorsons 1992

Design: Wheelhouse Creative

A catalogue record for this book
is available from the British Library

ISBN 0 00 713093 7

Printed and bound in Hong Kong

Contents

Kama Sutra

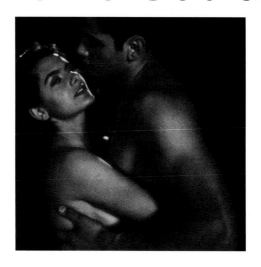

is a way of expressing love, pleasure and sensual

gratification

Introduction

'*After reading and considering the works of Babhravya and other ancient authors, and thinking over the meaning of the rules given by them, this treatise was composed, according to the precepts of the Holy Writ, for the benefit of the world, by Vatsyayana, while leading the life of a religious student at Benares, and wholly engaged in the contemplation of the Deity.*'

The *Kama Sutra* is the most famous book on lovemaking ever written. Originally composed by an Indian sage sometime between the fourth century BC and the first century AD, it was not translated into English until the 1880s, and has only been available to the general reader since the 1960s.

Not much is known about the author of the *Kama Sutra*. He belonged to the Vatsyayana sept, and his own name was Mallanaga. He embarked on the book as he was nearing the end of his life, and saw the writing of it as part of his religious duties. It is a learned and

carefully researched work, objective and semi-scientific, and is itself based on the writings of earlier sages.

The *Kama Sutra* was written at a time when a cultured Hindu was expected to acquire three 'principles': D*harma*, or religious merit, A*rtha*, or worldly wealth and *Kama*, the science of love and pleasure. Vatsyayana emphasises that 'this work is not to be used merely as an instrument for satisfying our desires'. However, it became, over the years, an essential part of the reading of thousands of Indians, and unlike other authors who wrote exclusively for men, Vatsyayana's classic book was used to instruct young brides before their weddings.

We owe much to the Victorian scholar and explorer Richard Burton and his associate Foster Arbuthnot, who took great pains to translate the original Sanskrit.

In the face of opposition and risking prosecution, they published it in 1883 under the fictitious imprint *The Kama Shastra Society of London and Benares*. It was circulated, with other translations of Eastern texts such as *The Perfumed Garden*, the *Ananga Ranga* and *The Arabian Nights*, among an elite group of people who were interested in the customs and behaviour of the Orient, although undoubtedly it was also used as a manual for Victorian husbands. Since it was discovered, the *Kama Sutra* revolutionized the Western approach to Indian culture, showing as it does how central and natural sex was to Indian thought.

The Sanskrit term *Kama* meant 'love, pleasure, sensual gratification', while *Sutra* meant 'aphorisms, compressed expressions' – a way of expressing complicated doctrines often used in early Sanskrit texts. But Kama is far more than just erotic pleasure. It encompasses all sensory pleasures. Thus good food, silken clothes, perfumes, music and painting all came within Kama's realm. When Vatsyayana named his treatise '*Kama Sutra*', he intended to lay down ideals for the enjoyment of all these pleasures. So he describes how the house of the ideal citizen is to be built, furnished and provisioned. Which sweet scented flowers should be grown in the gardens. With which paintings and sculptures the

rooms should be adorned, what incenses should perfume the air and what music should attend the meetings of lovers.

In a very real sense, sex was considered by the Hindus not only natural and necessary, but almost sacramental – the human counterpart of the miracle of creation. Erotic statues and carvings all over India testify to the fact that it was a subject to be approached with reverence and objectivity, rather than as something obscene and secret.

The *Kama Sutra* in its entirety is a long work and consists not only of detailed advice on the sexual act itself – in the section of the book known as 'the 64' – but also lays down instructions on courtship, marriage, education, household management, medicine, and various accomplishments cultured men and women needed to acquire in order to attract the opposite sex. Other chapters, such as those on prostitutes and courtesans, ritualized violence, the seduction of virgins and other men's wives, the use of go-betweens and harems, and the inherent racism and sexism, strike us today as irrelevant and, in parts, morally unacceptable. Taken as a whole, though, they give a fascinating picture of a dead civilisation – a formalized world of pleasure-gardens and palaces, of beautiful scented women, hedonistic courtiers and irrational, polygamous kings. A world, moreover, in which sexual expertise was elevated to a high art.

In India the *Kama Sutra* is still regarded as being of contemporary value, because its essence is not pleasure that comes from outside. It is about the enjoyment that comes from within – the pleasure to be had from two bodies and minds.

The *Kama Sutra* introduces us to a wide variety of sexual techniques and lovemaking positions, or 'asanas'. Some demand a fairly high degree of acrobatic ingenuity, and others require a flexibility that our rigid Western bodies are not used to, so please do take care. We have inevitably had to be selective in the positions we have chosen to illustrate here, but we are confident that those featured will provide a wonderfully varied and exciting way into the mysteries of the *Kama Sutra*. For the positions not covered here we have included sections from Burton's translation and from the Arab classic *The Perfumed Garden*, which was written in a quite different style but nevertheless gives details of many exotic and fascinating postures. The *Kama Sutra* is not pornography, nor is it a sex manual. It is a work of art, making skilful use of the Sanskrit language to convey different levels of meaning, both practical and philosophical, physical and metaphysical. It is as much about the spiritual side of love and sex as it is about exploring new exotic possibilities.

The writer of the *Kama Sutra* knew something that we have perhaps forgotten: that the sexual union of two people is an event far more profound than just pleasure-seeking. Again and again in the terse Sanskrik stanzas of the *Kama Sutra*, we encounter hints and clues of something deeper.

The text for this edition is a blend of two elements. Excerpts from Burton's translation give a flavour of the formality and aphoristic nature of the original, while the explanatory text is adapted from the script of the Vision video, a collaboration between Indra Sinha and Zek and Misha Halu, sex therapists, healers and specialists in ancient oriental sexual arts.

Although the focus is on heterosexual relationships, many of the general recommendations apply equally to gay and lesbian relationships. Furthermore, with the prevalence of AIDS and other sexually transmitted disease you are risking your life, and your partner's life, if you do not practise safe sex. This book is designed to be used as an adjunct to a loving, monogamous relationship.

The Kama Sutra Then and Now

Nearly two thousand years ago, in an Indian city halfway across the world, an old man sat down to write a book. He began by telling a story that was already thousands of years old, even in his day.

The great god Shiva, terrible destroyer of world, the ultimate teacher of all yoga, meditation and magic, was in the mood for love. Shiva and his wife, the beautiful goddess Parvati, locked themselves away in their room in their palace on Mount Kailash.

A year passed, and another, and the divine couple did not emerge. Ten thousand years went by and still they remained secluded. Only Nandi, the white bull, on guard outside the doors of their room, knew what was happening within.

What was happening was lovemaking of a kind that most human

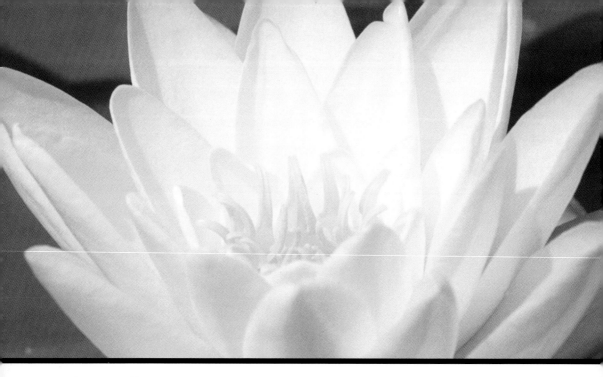

beings will never experience. Lovemaking that annihilates time. Of these things, Nandi was sworn never to speak.

But he could not help himself. What he had overheard was so overwhelming that it could by no means be kept secret. But even as Nandi broke his vow and spoke, the words turned to flowers that dropped from his mouth. These flowers were collected together and strung on threads, and wise men meditating upon them composed the first ever texts on lovemaking.

This first book was so huge that it would have made even the mighty *Decline and Fall of the Roman Empire* look like a footnote. So it was abbreviated. Once, then twice, then many times more. Teams of sages, working over a thousand years, condensed and condensed the sacred love teachings.

At last, at a time when the Roman empire was indeed hastening to decline, the entire Indian love tradition was distilled into a mere 4,000 stanzas – by one Mallanaga Vatsyayana.

He called his book *Kama Sutra*.

Kama Sutra, the Arts of Love. It remains to this day, the most famous – and the most potent – work on lovemaking ever written.

Vatsyayana's world, situated in the India of, probably, the fourth century AD, could hardly be more different from ours. It was a world of arrogant kings and chariot armies, of beauties locked harems, of rich urban playboys and skilled courtesans. But although music, drama and art all reached new heights in this era, many of its social attitudes strike us today as unacceptable.

So what is it that still lures us? After all, there are plenty of modern lovemaking manuals – why do we still turn with such fascination to a book written nearly two thousand years ago?

Perhaps because the subjects it deals with – love, sex, the body – are as relevant to us today as the day Vatsyayana first put pen to paper.

After all, the human body has not changed in the last two millennia. Nor the human emotions: love, fear, pleasure, anger and desire. Lovemaking is the only human activity that can transcend all cultures, all ages, all philosophies and all manners.

This book shows couples making love in some of the postures advocated by the *Kama Sutra*. But don't be fooled into thinking that it's the postures that are important. They're not. On its own, each posture is as meaningless as a single note of music – its value in a piece of music is determined by its relationship to other notes that come before and after.

Lovemaking should flow like music, one position changing easily and effortlessly to the next. To do this takes practice. You don't need to use every technique illustrated here; nor is it the physical performance that's really important. What matters is the feeling that we put into our lovemaking. Every action, every sound, every caress, every part of our body should express our affection, our tenderness, our loving care for our partner.

The mind is the most powerful sex organ of all. The forever-shifting, changing postures, flowing like dance figures from one to another, are expressions of the tenderness of the controlling mind. And for this reason, the *Kama Sutra* is especially valuable to couples who are married, or who are committed to each other in a long-term relationship.

Vatsyayana wrote that, properly practised, the arts of his *Kama Sutra* are so powerful that the love they arouse will not diminish, even in a thousand years.

The Kama Sutra in Practice

'When both the man and the woman afford mutual pleasure to each other…such is called a connection in the proper sense of the word.'

A bath taken together is one of the best ways to begin a lovemaking session. It allows you to touch each other's bodies with affection rather than passion. Passion comes later. It permits you to play games.

Kama is often translated as desire. But it is far more than just sexual pleasure.

Kama is all sensual pleasure, the delight of all five senses, of sight and sound, of touch and taste and smell.

Kama is the delight of seeing your lover's body. The smell of his, or her, hair. The delicious sensation of skin touching skin.

Ask the question, 'What is lovemaking?' and many people will immediately think of intercourse. But real sex, the lovemaking taught by the ancient texts, begins long before even arousal.

Lovemaking is the time spent just being together. Walking, talking or meditating. Sitting reading in the same room, or to one another. Singing together. And, or course, caring for one another's bodies.

It is above all expressing feelings of affection and care. When you touch one another's bodies, pay attention to what you are doing, be aware of every little action. One of the great secrets of lovemaking is very simple: slow down. Whatever you are doing, it will be better at half the speed.

Nothing heightens desire like expectation. Let your every touch contain a new idea, and let each contact burn like a cool fire.

In the bath, you may tease and tantalize, building an appetite for the more intense pleasure to come.

Embracing and making love in the water is called **Varikrida** – the Water Game.

Having bathed, your bodies are clean and sweet-scented, refreshed and relaxed. Even though you may be ready for making love, be patient just a little longer. You have still hardly begun to experience the pleasure that Kama has in store for you.

In Vatsyayana's day, they were as fond as we are today of exotic perfumes. Then, as now, it was an exquisite pleasure to be massaged with fragrant oils, such as jasmine, sandalwood, musk, ylang ylang, bergamot and thyme.

The simplest form of massage involves simply rubbing the scented oils into your lover's skin. If you are prepared to learn, there are various styles of massage, many of which are very beneficial to health. And, of course, sex will be so much better when every muscle is relaxed. Whatever the form of massage you practise, try to keep it non-sexual for as long as you can.

The art of enjoying Kama is to be able to recognize and experience to the full all the many different sorts of pleasure.

Those who become lovers of extreme skill never forget that the greatest enjoyment is the pleasure of caring for one another.

'In the pleasure room, decorated with flowers, and fragrant with perfumes...the citizen should receive the woman, who will come bathed and dressed, and should invite her to take refreshment and to drink freely. He should then seat her on his left side, and holding her hair, and touching also the end and knot of her garment, he should gently embrace her with his right arm. They should then carry on an amusing conversation on various subjects, and may also talk suggestively of things which would be considered as coarse, or not to be mentioned generally in society.'

They may then sing, either with or without gesticulations, and play on musical instruments, talk about the arts, and persuade each other to drink.
At last when the woman is overcome with love and desire, and the two are left alone, they should proceed as the Kama Sutra describes.'

Love-making does not, of course, only have to take place in the bedroom, but the Kama Sutra teaches that atmosphere is all-important. Use soft cushions and rugs, candles or low lighting to create a warm and intimate environment to relax in, freeing you from cares to explore each other's bodies.

'The following are the places for kissing: the forehead, the eyes, the cheeks, the throat, the bosom, the breasts, the lips and the interior of the mouth. Moreover, the people of the Lat country kiss also the following places: the joints of the thighs, the arms and the navel.'

According to ancient Indian – and Chinese – tradition, the body is made up of seven major energy centres called 'chakras' (see illustration opposite). At the base of the spine an awesome energy lies coiled. It is called Kundalini. It is roused by lovemaking, but its effects go far beyond. The effect of raising energy in the body, the ancients believed, was to fortify one's spiritual, emotional, mental and physical health. To do this, the energy of Kundalini, once aroused, had to be made to flow around from chakra to chakra, energizing and vitalizing as it went.

Some schools taught that the raising and control of Kundalini was a way to ultimate salvation – to Moksha – or release from the cycle of love and death. Moksha: the same word is used to describe the female orgasm.

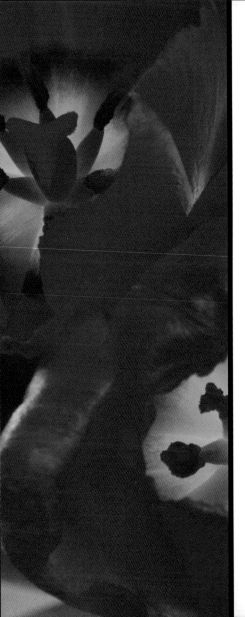

Now we come to the postures for which the *Kama Sutra* is famous. Again, remember they are not important in themselves, only as part of an ever-changing dance. The music for this dance is the flow of desire between you. Like dancers you have to be in control, yet at the same time completely lose yourself in the music.

When the urge to join your bodies becomes over-whelming, then choose a posture to start with and just go with the flow of your feelings.

Utphallaka – the Opening Flower. More usually referred to as the 'missionary' position, this is a good position to start in. She lies on her back, legs apart and feet lifted well off the cushions. It is a beautiful posture, allowing satisfying deep penetration and warm, affectionate contact of the upper body.

And from the simple start, see what a lovely line of postures flows. If she lifts her legs up high, if necessary steadying her own thighs with her hands, it becomes **Vijrimbhitaka** – the Widely Yawning. Even deeper, more intimate penetration and powerful sensation. Slow, deep strokes of the penis, more pressing than thrusting, yield great pleasure.

Indrani – the position tradition ascribes to the wife of the god Indra, arrived at by a further simple move as she brings her knees to her own shoulders. This posture shortens the vagina and is very intense. The man should be careful not to thrust too hard in case he hurts her, taking his cue from her.

He takes hold of her feet and presses them to his chest, in the most intense of this sequence of postures. It is called **Ratisundara** – Sweet Love – and calls for great skill on the part of the man in the way he uses his penis. Kneeling gives the man tremendous power to vary the depth and direction of his thrusts. In this posture he rotates his hips as he thrusts into her.

This posture is called **Bhugnaka** – the Rising. She lifts her legs up high, keeping them tightly squeezed together. If possible she should lift her buttocks off the floor so that her knees are near his shoulders. The man now feels the intensity of this posture, for when she presses her thighs together, his penis is trapped and deliciously squeezed.

The *Kama Sutra* enumerates many ways that the man can move his penis in the vagina. Short fluttering strokes have the strange name of **Chatakavilasa** – the Sporting of a Sparrow! But deep, circular motions give the posture variant its name: **Smarachakra** – Love's Wheel, which is said to be a great favourite with passionate women.

Piditaka – the Squeeze, intensifies the pressure as she crosses her raised thighs. This causes a marvellous sensation which can be made even more powerful if she now also squeezes with the muscles of her vagina.

By hooking her feet over his shoulders she opens up into the deep penetration posture known as **Jrimbhitaka** – the Yawning.

Now she unhooks one leg and stretches it out along the bed, leaving the other foot on his shoulder. This is followed by lifting the first leg back and stretching out the second along the bed, alternating slowly. This is the famous **Venudaritaka** – Splitting the Bamboo. By alternately lowering and stretching one leg at a time, her vagina rolls and squeezes, massaging the penis in a most particular way. It is one of the great secrets of Indian lovemaking, yet so absurdly simple when you know how.

She then draws both feet down, leaving them apart, then slowly draws them together under his body and squeezes them tight, his legs now falling outside hers.

Lying with her legs apart beneath him, she brings them slowly and deliberately together beneath his. His legs are forced up and over the outside of hers and she captures and squeezes his penis with her vaginal muscles.

Hold it for a breath of ten beats, then relax and open up again. Do it again. And again. It is called **Samputa** – the Box, and it feels sensational.

'The inner room should be occupied by the females, while the outer room, balmy with rich perfumes, should contain a bed, soft, agreeable to the sight, covered with a clean white cloth, low in the middle part, having garlands and bunches of flowers upon it, and two pillows, one at the top, another at the bottom. There should be also a sort of couch besides and at the head of this a sort of stool, on which should be placed the fragrant ointments for the night, as well as flowers, pots containing collyrium and other fragrant substances, things used for perfuming the mouth, and the bark of the common citron tree.'

The bedroom is the place in our home where lovemaking usually takes place. Usually we get into bed together and, before going to sleep, cuddle a little and soon find ourselves having intercourse. But lovemaking – like any art – needs to be practised. Think of your bodies as musical instruments. You need to practise before you can play beautiful music with them.

'When love becomes intense, pressing with the nails or scratching the body with them is practised. It is employed, together with biting, by those to whom the practice is agreeable. Pressing with the nails is of the eight following kinds, according to the forms of the marks which are produced: Sounding – Half Moon – A Circle – A Line – A tiger's nail or claw – A peacock's foot – The jump of a hare – The leaf of a blue lotus.

The places that are to be pressed with the nails are as follows: the armpit, the throat, the breasts, the lips, the jaghana, or middle parts of the body, and the thighs. But Suvarnanadbha is of the opinion that the impetuosity of passion is excessive, the places need not be considered...

When a person presses the chin, the breasts, the lower lip, or the jaghana or another so softly that no scratch or mark is left, but only the hair on the body becomes erect from the touch of the nails, and the nails themselves make a sound, it is called a "sounding or pressing with the nails".'

Giving names to each nail mark, tooth mark and sexual posture might seem to you to be somewhat unspontaneous. But there was another reason for not giving way – for a long time at least – to unbridled passion.

According to the Indian Tantrics and the Chinese Taoists too, ejaculation was to be avoided in order to prolong lovemaking indefinitely. With practice, they could maintain a near-orgasmic state for hours.

By slowing everything down, when the orgasm finally comes, you may find that you can feel it in every part of your body, from your back and neck to your calves and even the soles of your feet.

'At the first time of sexual union the passion of the male is intense, and his time is short, but in subsequent unions on the same day the reverse of this is the case. With the female however it is the contrary, for at the first time her passion is weak, and then her time long, but on subsequent occasions on the same day, her passion is intense and her time short, until her passion is satisfied.'

A medieval Sanskrit text, *Ratiratnapradipika*, which has never been translated into English, gives the eight ancient Indian techniques of cunnilingus. These include licking of the clitoris with the tongue – up and down the clitoris hood, in tiny circles, probing deeply with the tongue into the vagina. By sucking up her inner lips and clitoris into his mouth a man can create exquisite sensations for a woman. You can suck hard and perhaps even nip a little, but with very great care since the clitoris is very sensitive. With all these techniques it is important to find out what she likes and dislikes.

'A man should gather from the actions of the woman of what disposition she is, and in what way she likes to be enjoyed.'

'When one of her legs is placed on the head, and the other is stretched out, it is called "fixing of a nail". This is learnt by practice only.

When both the legs of the woman are contracted, and placed on her stomach, it is called the "crab's position".

When the thighs are raised and placed one upon the other, it is called the "packed position".

When the shanks are placed one upon the other, it is called the "lotus-like position".'

When you are both well aroused and ready, then perhaps try this slightly more advanced sequence of postures:

Ratibana – Love's Arrow – is a delightful posture, which gives deep and easy penetration and is very close and loving. He raises one of her feet up high, pressing it to his chest, her other leg stretched out straight.

By moving one of her feet the couple are in the posture known as **Vinasana** – the Lute – particularly adored by experienced women, says the poet of the *Ananga Ranga*. The penetration here is deeper and more intense.

To maintain the deep, close union, he can rock backwards and forwards, hardly moving his penis within her. This is a technique much in favour with the Tantrics and Taoists, said to be another of the infallible ways to engender love.

By twisting round onto her face from the previous position, she transforms it into the rear entry position **Ekabandha** – the Knot. He kneels behind her with her hips pulled right back into his lap, giving very close intimacy, deep penetration and easy control…

'When a man, during congress, turns round, and enjoys the woman without leaving her, while she embraces him around the back all the time, it is called the "turning position", and is learnt only by practice.'

By varying the angle at which he strikes in with his penis, he can massage her G-spot, the sensitive region which lies about two inches inside the vagina.

The *Kama Sutra* teaches that the degree of a lover's skill is determined by how far he or she can prolong the pleasure of making love. One way, when passion threatens to overwhelm you, is to regulate the rhythm of your breathing, with slow, deep breaths.

Kirtibandha – the Famous Knot – is a relatively simple posture which cannot be bettered for deep, intimate penetration and just for being close. She sits astride his lap, her legs wrapped around his waist.

Lifting her knees up, with her weight on her feet and holding the headboard for support, the position becomes **Bhramara** – the Bee. It gives the woman complete control, allowing her to vary the direction, depth and rhythm of the penetration. Her swirling movements mimic those of a bee delving for pollen in a flower.

Then, by moving one foot to his chest, it becomes **Hansa Lila** – the Sporting of Swans. This opens her up more and enables her to send his penis almost anywhere she likes inside her pelvis.

Moving both feet to one side of him, and supporting herself if necessary on her elbows on his other side, we have **Hansabandha** – a second position named for the Swan. This is not particularly easy to master, but gives a unique sensation as the angle of the penis and vagina diverge: another good position for finding the G-spot.

By resting the foot nearest his feet on one of his ankles, she reaches the **Garuda** posture. This in turn can be twisted into **Pravrittaka** – the Turnaround, in which she turns herself round to face his feet, reaches out and grasps them. This is a virtuoso move that can only be learned through practice. Not only does it afford deep and comfortable penetration but gives her lover a most erotic view of her buttocks repeatedly swallowing up his penis.

'The signs of the enjoyment and satisfaction of the woman are as follows: her body relaxes, she closes her eyes, she puts aside all bashfulness, and shows increased willingness to unite the two organs as closely together as possible.'

'When lovers lie on a bed, and embrace each other so closely that the arms and thighs of the one are encircled by the arms and thighs of the other, and are, as it were, rubbing up against them, this is called an embrace like "the mixture of sesamum seed with rice."

When a man and a woman are very much in love with each other and, not thinking of any pain or hurt, embrace each other as if they were entering into each other's bodies, either while the woman is sitting on the lap of the man, or in front of him, or on a bed, then it is called an embrace like a "mixture of milk and water".'

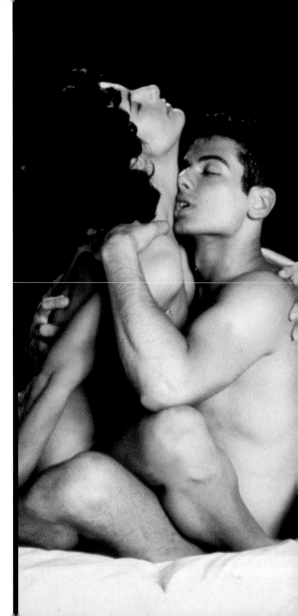

'Passionate actions and amorous gesticulations or movements, which arise on the spur of the movement, and during sexual intercourse, cannot be defined, and are as irregular as dreams. A horse having once attained the fifth degree of motion goes on with blind speed, regardless of pits, ditches, and posts in his way, and in the same manner a loving pair become blind with passion in the heat of congress, and go on with great impetuosity, paying not the least regard to excess. For this reason one who is well acquainted with the science of love, and knowing his own strength, as also the tenderness, impetuosity and strength of the young woman, should act accordingly.'

There will be times when passion creeps up on you when you are least expecting it and is so overwhelming that it cannot be denied. Acting impetuously, on the spur of the moment, can, it would seem, be as inconvenient as it is exciting, so it is a good idea to know a few techniques that will be useful when, like lightning, passion strikes.

'When a girl only touches the mouth of her lover with her own, but does not herself do anything, it is called the "nominal kiss". When a girl, setting aside her bashfulness a little, wishes to touch the lip that is pressed into her mouth, and with that object moves her lower lip, but not the upper one, it is called the "throbbing kiss". When a girl touches her lover's lip with her tongue, and having shut her eyes, places her hands on those of her lover, it is called the "touching kiss". When the lips of two lovers are brought into direct contact with each other, it is called a "straight kiss". When the heads of the two lovers are bent towards each other, and when so bent, kissing takes place, it is called a "bent kiss". When one of them turns up the face of the other by holding the head and chin, and then kissing, it is called a "turned kiss". Lastly, when the lower lip is pressed with much force, it is called a "pressed kiss".'*

Boisterous lovemaking, especially when using hard surfaces such as a table instead of soft cushions, can sometimes cause bumps and bruises. But as Vatsyayana observes, when we are alone and see again the marks of passion on our bodies, feelings of love come welling up afresh.

Postures that involve the use of a table can give deep easy access. **Vymonapada** – the Sky Foot – is a good example. She lies back on the table, gripping the edges for support and raising her legs as he enters her. It is a position in which hard, passionate blows of the penis may be struck. If she enjoys it, he may try withdrawing completely, and then striking in, hard, to the full length of his penis. This is called **Nirghata** – the Buffet. It can be varied by her slightly crossing her legs and placing both heels on one of his shoulders, an elegant posture which enables him to keep up the pressure against one wall of her vagina. This is **Varahaghata** – the Boar's Thrust.

Sitting on the very edge of the table with her heels on the rim and with her arms locked around his neck gives a position that affords very deep penetration. As this may be a little uncomfortable for her, in order to press in closely and delay ejaculation he may hold his penis pressed breathlessly in as deep as it will go. This technique is known as **Piditaka** – Pressing.

From this position she locks her legs completely around his waist and he lifts her off completely, converting the posture to a standing one. Known as **Avalambitaka** – Suspended, this is a simple move to get into, but one that can be quite difficult to hold for long.

When the position can no longer be held, move to a chair. Sitting on a chair he disengages her feet from behind his back and puts his feet on the ground – using the leverage to control the depth, speed and direction of his thrusts.

She then puts her feet on the ground, and swings her hips around. This is **Dolita** – the Swing. To move to **Kshudgara** – the Striking – she lifts her feet up a little, increasing the depth and angle of his penis within her while still retaining complete control of her own movements.

By lifting her feet up on to the sides of the chair she is completely opened to him and yet still able to vary the rhythm and depth of her thrusts down on him. Five shallow and one deep thrust, for instance, is a technique much praised by Taoists.

By placing her feet on the floor and turning her back to him she sheathes the penis deeply in her vagina. She can now use her muscles to grip and squeeze it. If she squeezes hard as she very slowly lets it withdraw, as though 'milking' it with her vagina, then it is known as **Vadavaka** – the Mare, which is only learned by practice.

'Acts to be done by the man:
   When the organs are brought together properly and directly it is called "moving the organ forward".
   When the lingam is held with the hand, and turned all round in the yoni, it is called "churning".
   When the yoni is lowered and the upper part of it is struck with the lingam, it is called "piercing".
   When the same thing is done on the lower part of the yoni, it is called "rubbing".
   When the yoni is pressed by the lingam for a long time, it is called "pressing".
   When both sides of the yoni are rubbed in this way, it is called the "blow of a bull".'

'Acts to be done by the woman:
   When the woman holds the lingam in her yoni, draws it in, presses it, and keeps it thus in her for a long time, it is called the "pair of tongs".
   When, while engaged in congress, she turns round like a wheel, it is called the "top". This is learnt by practice only.
   When the woman is tired, she should place her forehead on that of her lover, and should thus take rest without disturbing the union of the organs, and when the woman has rested herself the man should turn round and begin the congress again.'

* The terms lingam and yoni are ancient Eastern terms referring to the male and female genitalia respectively.

'In the garden...plant beds of green vegetables, bunches of sugar cane, and clumps of fig tree, the mustard plant, the parsley plant and the fennel plant. Clusters of various flowers such as the wild jasmine, the yellow amaranth, Arabian and Spanish jasmines, the frangipani, and the fragrant white flower called the Queen of the Night should likewise be planted, together with flowering groves of Indian coral and catechu trees, banana palms and tall strands of fresh-smelling khus khus grass. Footpaths should lead from the house and wander between the flowers and trees. In the garden there should also be a whirling swing and a common swing, as also a bower of creepers covered with flowers, in which a raised parterre should be made for sitting.'

The ideal garden for the third century citizen was a place to relax, and a place to make love in. If you are lucky enough to have a garden of your own, private and not overlooked, you can use it to enhance your lovemaking.

The objective of the postures and techniques advocated by the *Kama Sutra* is not to acquire virtuosity but to build love between husband and wife.

'When holding the man's lingam with her hand, and placing it between her lips, the woman moves about her mouth, it is called the "nominal congress".

When covering the end of the lingam with her fingers collected together like the bud of a plant or flower, the woman presses the sides of it with her lips, using her teeth also, it is called "biting the sides".

When the woman presses the end of the lingam with her lips closed together, and kisses it as if she were drawing it out, it is called the "outside pressing".

When she puts the lingam further into her mouth, and presses it with her lips and then takes it out, it is called the "inside pressing".

When, holding the lingam in her hand, the woman kisses it as if she were kissing the lower lip, it is called "kissing".

When, after kissing it, she touches it with her tongue everywhere, and passes the tongue over the end of it, it is called "rubbing".

When, in the same way, she puts the half of it into her mouth, and forcibly kisses and sucks it, this is called "sucking a mango".

And lastly, when the woman puts the whole lingam into her mouth, and presses it to the very end, as if she were going to swallow it up, it is called "swallowing up".'

The *Kama Sutra*, and all the India love texts that followed it, always reserved a special pride of place for the standing postures, which were thought difficult and therefore especially splendid. They were called 'picture positions' because these were the postures chosen by sculptors to adorn temple walls.

In the embrace opposite he supports her knees with his elbows: this posture is known as **Janukurpara** – Knee Elbow.

Her foot then travels up his body to his thigh. This is known as **Vriksha** – the Climbing of a Tree.

She is now in **Ekapada** – One Foot. From this position he can bend down and lift up her other leg and support her on his elbows, transforming the posture into **Janukurpara**.

In another version of **Dolita** – the Swing, he leans against the tree while she works her feet round to place her soles flat against the trunk, gently pushing herself backwards and forwards.

By broadening his stance out he achieves the posture called the Tree. With practice it is possible to maintain it for very long periods, important to Chinese Taoists and Indian Tantrics alike, whose aim was to make intercourse last as long as possible.

We now move to **Gardhaba** – the Ass. This is a very close, intimate way of coupling, giving intense pleasure to both partners. She stands with her back to him, he bends his knees and takes her from behind. This is a position which can be seen on the walls of many Khajuraho temples.

'An ingenious person should multiply the kinds of congress after the fashion of the different kinds of beasts and birds. For these different kinds of congress, performed according to the usage of each country, and the liking of the individual, generate love, friendship and respect in the hearts of women.'

Turning around again she lifts one foot up high in his palm, opening up wide to him. This is **Tala** – the palm, a sensual and beautiful posture that can also easily be performed using a chair.

Pushing her feet against the tree trunk, she can make the transition into **Avalambitaka** – Suspended, which enables her to rock her hips back and forth against him.

Tripdadam – the Tripod. Letting her foot drop down he catches her knee, ending up with three feet on the ground.

'When a woman, clinging to a man as a creeper twines round a tree, bends his head down to hers with the desire of kissing him and slightly makes the sound of sut sut, embraces him, and looks lovingly towards him, it is called an embrace like the "twining of a creeper".

When a woman, having placed one of her feet on the foot of her lover, and the other on one of his thighs, passes one of her arms round his back, and the other on his shoulders, makes slightly the sounds of singing and cooing, and wishes, as it were, to climb up him in order to have a kiss, it is called an embrace like the "climbing of a tree".

These two kinds of embrace take place when the lover is standing.'

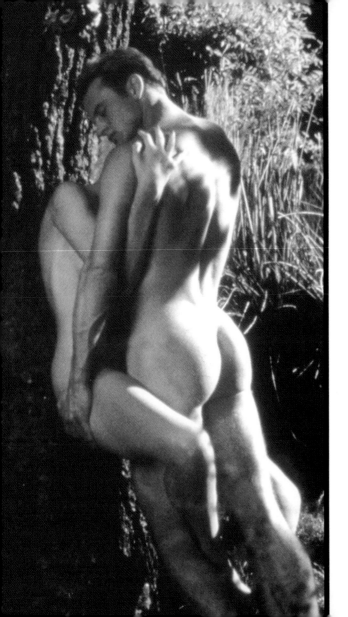

For the ancient
Indians, lovemaking
went beyond the
merely human and
mortal. It touched the
divine itself. No
coincidence perhaps
that a story that began
with a god and
goddess locked away in
a ten thousand year
passion should end
with a posture
dedicated to another
god: for this lovely,
natural position is
called **Traivikrama**,
the Stride of Vishnu,
after the god Vishnu
who covered the earth
in three strides.

Vatsyayana concluded the *Kama Sutra* with the following flourish:

'A man, employing the sixty-four means mentioned by Babhravya, obtains his object, and enjoys the woman of the first quality. Though he may speak well on other subjects, if he does not know the sixty-four divisions, no great respect is paid to him in the assembly of the learned. A man, devoid of other knowledge, but well acquainted with the sixty-four divisions, becomes a leader in any society of men and women...As the sixty-four arts are respected, are charming, and add to the talent of women, they are called by the Acharyas dear to women.'

Richard Burton, sensing perhaps that the lengthy work he had laboured over for so long was to become known as one of the world's great books, ended his translation with Shakespeare's moving elegiac couplet:

So long as lips shall kiss, and eyes shall see, So long lives This, and This gives life to Thee.

More Positions

Many more sexual positions and techniques are described in *The Perfumed Garden*, another classic work on lovemaking from the ancient East. Originally written by Sheikh Nefzawi, this too was translated by Richard Burton. We have included a selection here, as they admirably complement those in the *Kama Sutra*.

Concerning the Different Postures for Coition

The ways of uniting with woman are numerous and varied, and the time has arrived when you should learn the different postures. God has said: 'Woman is your field, go to your field with a will!' (*Koran*). According to your taste you may choose the posture which pleases you most, provided always that intercourse takes place through the appointed organ: the yoni.

First Posture: Lay the woman on her back and raise her thighs, then, getting between her legs, introduce your lingam. Gripping the ground with your toes, you will be able to move in a suitable manner. This posture is a good one for those who have long members.

Second Posture: If your lingam is short, lay the woman on her back and raise her legs in the air so that her toes touch her ears. Her buttocks being thus raised, the yoni is thrown forward. Now introduce your lingam.

Third Posture: Lay the woman on the ground and get between her thighs; then, putting one of her legs on your shoulder and the other under your arm, penetrate her.

Fourth Posture: Stretch the woman on the ground and put her legs on your shoulders; in that position your lingam will be exactly opposite her yoni which will be lifted off the ground. That is the moment for introducing your lingam.

Fifth Posture: Let the woman lie on her side on the ground; then, lying down yourself and getting between her thighs, introduce your lingam. This posture is apt to give rise to rheumatic or sciatic pains.

Sixth Posture: Let the woman rest on her knees and elbows in the position for prayer. In this position the yoni stands out behind.

Seventh Posture: Lay the woman on her side, and then you yourself sitting on your heels will place her top leg on your nearest shoulder and her other leg against your thighs. She will keep on her side and you will be between her legs. Introduce your lingam and move her backwards and forwards with your hands.

Eighth Posture: Lay the woman on her back and kneel astride her.

Ninth Posture: Place the woman so that she rests, either face forward or the reverse, against a slightly raised platform, her feet remaining on the ground and her body projecting in front. She will thus present her yoni to your lingam which you will introduce.

Tenth Posture: Place the woman on a rather low divan and let her grasp the woodwork with her hands. Then, placing her legs on your hips and telling her to grip your body with them, you will introduce your lingam, at the same time grasping the divan. When you begin to work, let your movements keep time.

Eleventh Posture: Lay the woman on her back and let her buttocks be raised by a cushion placed under them. Let her put the soles of her feet together: now get between her thighs.

There are other postures besides the preceding in use in India. It is well that you should know that the Hindus have greatly multiplied the ways of possessing a woman and have carried their investigations in this matter much further than the Arabs. Among other postures and variations are the following:

The Closure: Lay the woman on her back and raise her buttocks with a cushion; then get between her legs, keeping your toes on the floor, and force her thighs against her chest. Now pass your hands under her arms to clasp her to you, or tightly grip her shoulders. That done, introduce your lingam and draw her towards you at the moment of ejaculation. This posture is painful for the woman, for, with her thighs pressed on her chest and her buttocks raised with the cushion, the walls of the vagina are forced together, and, as a consequence – the uterus being pushed forward – there is not enough room for the lingam which can only be inserted with difficulty, and which impinges on the womb. This posture should only be used when the lingam is short and soft.

The Frog's Posture: Place the woman on her back and raise her thighs till her heels are close to her buttocks. Now seat yourself in front of her yoni and introduce your lingam; then put her knees under your armpits and, grasping the upper part of her arms, draw her to you at the propitious moment.

The Clasping of Hands and Feet: Lay the woman on her back, then sit on your heels between her thighs and grip the floor with your toes; she will now put her legs round your body and you will put your arms about her neck.

The Raised Legs Posture: While the woman is lying on her back take hold of her legs and, holding them close together, raise them until her soles point to the ceiling; then clasping her between your thighs, introduce your lingam, taking care at the same time not to let her legs fall.

The Goat's Posture: Let the woman lie on her side and stretch out her bottom leg. Crouch down between her thighs, lift her top leg and introduce your lingam. Hold her by the arms or shoulders.

The Archimedean Screw: While the man is lying on his back the woman sits on his lingam, keeping her face towards his. She then places her hands on the bed, at the same time keeping her belly off his; she now moves up and down and, if the man is light in weight, he may move as well. If the woman wishes to kiss the man she need only lay her arms on the bed.

The Somersault: The woman should let her trousers fall to her ankles so that they are like fetters. She then bends down till her head is in her trousers, when the man, seizing her legs, pulls her over onto her back. He then kneels down and penetrates her. It is said that there are women, who, when lying on their back, can put their feet under their head without the help of their hands or trousers.

The Ostrich's Tail: Lay the woman on the ground and kneel at her feet; then raise her legs and place them round your neck so that only her head and shoulders remain on the ground. Now penetrate her.

Putting on the Sock: The woman being on her back, you sit between her legs and place your lingam between the lips of her yoni which you grasp with the thumb and first finger. You then move so that the part of your lingam which is in contact with the woman is subjected to rubbing, and continue so until her yoni is moist with the liquid which escapes from your penis. Having thus given her a foretaste of pleasure, you penetrate her completely.

The Mutual View of the Buttocks: The man lies on his back, and the woman, turning her back to him, sits on his lingam. He now clasps her body with his legs and she leans over until her hands touch the floor. Thus supported she has a view of his buttocks, and he of hers, and she is able to move conveniently.

Drawing the Bow: Let the woman lie on her side, and the man, also on his side, gets between her legs so that his face is turned towards her back; now, placing his hands on her shoulders, he introduces his lingam. The woman then grasps the man's feet and draws them towards her; she forms thus, with the man's body, a bow to which she is the arrow.

Reciprocating Motion: The man, seated on the ground, brings the soles of his feet together, at the same time lowering his thighs. The woman then sits on his feet and clasps his body with her legs and his neck with her arms. The man then grasps the woman's legs, and moving his feet towards his body, carries the woman within reach of his lingam, which he introduces. By a movement of his feet he now moves her backwards and forwards. The woman should take care to facilitate this movement by not pressing too heavily. If the man fears

that his lingam will be drawn right out, he must grasp the woman round the body and be satisfied with such movement as he can give with his feet.

Pounding the Spot: The man sits down and stretches out his legs, and the woman sits on his thighs and crosses her legs behind his back. She places her yoni opposite his lingam and lends a guiding hand. She then puts her arms round his neck, and he puts his round her waist and raises and lowers her on his lingam, in which movement she assists.

Coition from Behind: The woman lies face downwards and raises her buttocks with a cushion; the man lies on her back and introduces his lingam while she slips her arms through his elbows.

Belly to Belly: The man and woman stand face to face, the latter with her feet slightly apart, the man's feet being between. Both now advance their feet. The man should now place one foot in advance of the other, and each should clasp the other round the loins. The man then penetrates and both move in the manner explained on *page* 86 (see First Movement).

The Sheep's Posture: The woman kneels down and

puts her forearms on the ground; the man kneels down behind her and slips his lingam in her yoni which she makes stand out as much as possible. His hands should be placed on her shoulders.

The Camel's Hump: The woman, who is standing, bends forward till her fingers touch the floor; the man gets behind and copulates, at the same time grasping her thighs. If the man withdraws while the woman is still bending down, the yoni emits a noise like the bleating of a calf, and for that reason women object to the posture.

Driving in the Peg: While facing each other, the woman, hanging with her arms round the man's neck, raises her legs and with them clasps him round the waist, resting her feet against a wall. The man now introduces his lingam, and the woman is then as if hanging on a peg.

The Fusion of Love: The woman lies on her right side and the man on his left; the man stretches out his bottom leg straight down and raises the other leg, letting it rest on the woman's side. The woman now puts her top leg on the man's body and the lingam is introduced. The woman may help if she likes, to make the necessary movements.

Inversion: The man lies on his back and the woman lies on him. She grasps his thighs and draws them towards her, thus bringing his lingam into prominence. Having guided it in, she puts her hands on the bed, one on each side of the man's buttocks. It is necessary for her feet to be raised on a cushion to allow for the slope of the lingam. The woman moves. The posture may be varied by the woman sitting on her heels between the man's legs.

Riding the Lingam: The man lies down and places a cushion under his shoulders, taking care that his buttocks remain on the floor. Thus placed, he raises his legs till his knees are close to his face. The woman then sits on his lingam. She does not lie down but sits astride, as though on a saddle formed by the man's leg and chest. By bending her knees she can now move upwards and downwards; or, she may put her knees on the floor, in which case the man moves her with his thighs while she grasps his shoulders.

The Jointer: The man and woman sit down facing each other; the woman then puts her right thigh on the man's left thigh, and he puts his right thigh on her left one. The woman guides his lingam into her yoni and grasps the man's arms while he grasps hers. They now indulge in a see-saw motion, leaning backwards and forwards alternately, taking care that their movements are well timed.

The Stay-at-Home: The woman lies on her back, and the man, with

cushions under his hands, lies on her. When the introduction has taken place the woman raises her buttocks as far a possible from the bed, and the man accompanies her in the movement, taking care that his lingam is not withdrawn. The woman then drops her buttocks with short sharp jerks, and although the two are not clasped together, the man should keep quite close to the woman. They continue this movement, but it is necessary that the man be light and the bed soft; otherwise pain will be caused.

The Blacksmith's Posture: The woman lies on her back with a cushion under her buttocks. She draws her knees onto her chest so that her yoni stands out like a sieve; she then guides in the lingam. The man now performs for a moment or two the conventional movements. He then withdraws his lingam and slips it between the woman's thighs in imitation of the blacksmith who draws the hot iron from the fire and plunges it into cold water.

The Seductive Posture: The woman lies on her back and the man crouches between her legs which he then puts under his arms or on his shoulders. He may hold her by the waist or the arms.

I have not thought it necessary to mention those postures which appeared to me impossible of accomplishment and, if anyone should think the number given too small, he has nothing to do but invent more. It is incontestable that the Hindus have surmounted enormous difficulties in postures for coition; the following is an example: the woman lies on her back and the man sits astride her chest, facing towards her feet. He now bends forward and raises her thighs till her yoni is opposite the lingam which he then introduces. As you can see, this posture is difficult to execute and very tiring. I think it is only realisable in thought or design.

It is related that there are woman, who, during coition, can raise one of their legs in the air and balance a lighted lamp on the sole of their foot, without spilling the oil or extinguishing the lamp. Intercourse is not interfered with by this action which demands, however, great skill. Nevertheless, the things to be sought for most in copulation, those which give the greatest pleasure, are the embraces, the kisses, and the sucking of each other's lips. These differentiate man from the animals. No one is insensible to the pleasures which arise from difference of sex, and man's highest pleasure is copulation. When a man's love is carried to its highest pitch, all the pleasures of coition become easy for him, and he satisfies them by embracing and kissing. There is the real source of happiness for both.

It is advisable that the connoisseur of copulation should try all the postures so that he may know which gives pleasure to the woman. He will then adopt that for preference and will have the satisfaction of retaining the woman's affection. By universal consent pounding on the spot gives most satisfaction.

It remains for me now to speak of the different movements used in copulation.

First Movement: The Bucket in the Well. The man and woman embrace closely after penetration, then the man moves once and slightly draws back; the woman now moves and withdraws in her turn, and so on

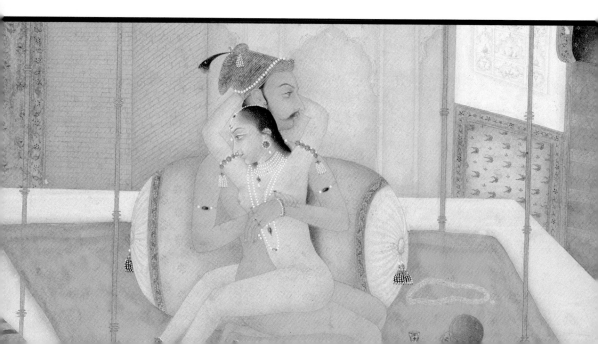

alternately. They should take care to place their hands and feet against each other's and imitate, as well they can, the descent of a bucket in a well.

Second Movement: The Mutual Shock. Both draw away after the introduction, taking care that the lingam is not entirely withdrawn; they then come together smartly and closely embrace. They continue thus.

Third Movement: Going Shares. The man moves in the usual manner, then stops; the woman, keeping the lingam in place, moves once then stops. The man now recommences, and so they continue till they ejaculate.

Fourth Movement: Love's Tailor. The man partly penetrates and moves with a rubbing motion; then, with a single stroke, he enters completely. Such is the action of a tailor who, after having inserted his needle, draws it through with a single pull. This movement is only suitable for those who can control their ejaculation.

Fifth Movement: The toothpick. The man introduces his lingam and explores the yoni from top to bottom and on all sides.

Sixth Movement: Love's Bond. The man penetrates completely so that his body is perfectly close to the woman's. He should now move energetically, taking care that not the smallest portion is withdrawn from the yoni. This is the best movement of all, and is particularly suitable for pounding the spot. Women prefer it to the exclusion of all others as it procures them the greatest pleasure, and allows the yoni to clasp the lingam. Tribads use no other movement, and it can be recommended to all who suffer from premature ejaculation.

Any posture is unsatisfactory if kissing is impossible; pleasure will be incomplete, for a kiss is one of the most potent stimulants of all.

It is claimed by some that kissing is an integral part of copulation. The most delightful kiss is that which is planted on moist ardent lips, and accompanied with suction of the lips and tongue, so that the emission of a sweet intoxicating saliva is produced. It is for the man to procure this emission from the woman by gently nibbling her lips and tongue till she secretes a particular saliva, sweet, exquisite, more agreeable than honey mixed with pure water, and which does not mix with her ordinary saliva. This gives the man a shivering sensation throughout his whole body, and is more intoxicating than strong wine. A kiss should be sonorous. Its sound, light and prolonged takes its rise between the tongue and the moist edge of the palate. It is produced by a movement of the tongue in the mouth and a displacement of the saliva provoked by suction. A kiss given on the outside of the lips and accompanied with a sound like that made when calling a cat, gives no pleasure whatever. Such a kiss is only meant for children, or the hands. The kiss which I have described above, and which belongs to copulation, provokes a delicious voluptuousness. It is for you to learn the difference.

Bibliography

It has not been possible in this edition to include the entire text of the Kama Sutra. However, the following editions are recommended:

The Kama Sutra, edited by WG Archer, Allen & Unwin 1965, Aquarian Press 1991

The Kama Sutra of Vatsyayana, edited by John Muirhead-Gould with an introduction by Dom Moraes, Grafton Books 1963

The Love Teachings of Kama Sutra, Trans. Indra Sinha, Hamlyn 1980

The Illustrated Kama Sutra, Anaga Ranga, Perfumed Garden, edited by Charles Fowkes, Hamlyn 1987